Jan 16, 2015

CLUTTER BUSTING for BUSY WOMEN

HOW TO CREATE A
C.A.L.M. LIFE TO
HAVE MORE TIME
& ENERGY

This book is being given to

Alana

because YOU, your happiness and
well-being, matter to me.

Much Love — Judi

More Praise for Virginia Barkley and
ClutterBusting for Busy Women

"If you are ready to be more productive, organized and energized, then read and use the strategies in this brilliant book by my friend Virginia Barkley!"

> – **James Malinchak,** Author, *Millionaire Success Secrets*
> Featured on ABC's hit TV show, "Secret Millionaire"
> Founder, www.BigMoneySpeaker.com

"Virginia's genuine regard for the well-being of others is evident! She demystifies clutter and gives readers simple tools that work and the confidence to break free from old habits that are not serving them well. The result ... clearer focus and happiness."

> – **Laurie Ann Goldman,** CEO, SPANX, Inc.

"This fast-moving, practical book shows you how to quickly simplify your life and eliminate all the clutter."

> – **Brian Tracy,** President, Brian Tracy International,
> Top-selling author of 70 books, including *Maximum Achievement: Strategies and Skills That Will Unlock Your Hidden Powers To Succeed,* www.BrianTracy.com

"*ClutterBusting for Busy Women* is insightful and empowering. Virginia shows readers how to clear space to make room for what really matters. More living. Less stuff. I have a new perspective and a confident outlook on my abilities to get and stay organized. Thank you, Virginia Barkley!"

> – **Barbara Niven,** Actress, " Hollywood's Top Media Trainer"
> Appeared in over 2,500 movies and television commercials
> www.BarbaraNiven.com

"I feel like Virginia wrote this for me. I read this book in one sitting and have already started implementing the C.A.L.M. tactics. Thank you for the insights and ideas!"

> – **Jill Lublin**, International speaker and three-time best-selling author of books, including *Guerilla Publicity*
> www.PublicityCrashCourse.com

"Wow! A real eye-opener if you want to learn the root causes of clutter and ways to prevent it from building up in the first place."

> – **Vicki Irvin**, CEO, Superwoman Lifestyle
> www.vickiirvin.com

"There are clutter-busters and there are rock star clutter-busters. Virginia Barkley is a rock star clutter-buster, and her new book, *ClutterBusting for Busy Women*, is the answer to streamline belongings and create sustainable organization in both our homes and our lives."

> – **Craig Duswalt**, Creator of the Rock Star System for Success and former personal manager for Axl Rose, lead singer of Guns 'N Roses
> www.CraigDuswalt.com

"Virginia Barkley is full of wisdom and inspiration that she shares generously in her wonderful book, *ClutterBusting for Busy Women*. Virginia walks us through so much more than simply organizing things. In this valuable book, she empowers women to organize our lives so we can focus on what is most important to us and free up our energy to be able to create our dreams. A great read for every woman!"

> – **Dr. Eve Agee, Ph.D.**, Best-selling author, *The Uterine Health Companion: The Holistic Guide To Lifelong Wellness*
> www.EveAgee.com

"As usual, Virginia makes what could be painful a whole lot of fun! She makes me look forward to organizing my stuff! Thanks Virginia for being so Vividly YOU!"

– **Leela Francis,** Founder, Vividly Woman, Embodied Leader & Coach Training, www.VividlyWoman.com

"This is a **must** read! Virginia offers practical advice and steps to improve your life today. Every busy woman I know can benefit from this book immediately so what are you waiting for? Make your own coffee a few days this week and invest that Starbucks money on something that will improve your life forever! Seriously, there are no excuses for a busy woman not to read this now! She has a gift and she is sharing it with you. Enjoy, you'll thank me and Virginia once you read it."

– **Paige Arnof-Fenn,** Founder and CEO, Mavens & Moguls www.MavensAndMoguls.com

"Virginia's passion for her clients and her work shine through her words. She has some *amazing* ideas. Listen to her."

– **Jonathan Sprinkles.** TV personality and award-winning speaker, www.GetAndStayMotivated.com

"If your bookshelves are cluttered with dozens of books on how to live better, find balance or be more productive – clear them away and put this ONE book in their place. It will change the way you think about your personal energy, your personal space and your connection to 'things.' It's a radical new way to relate to the 'stuff' in your life that will bring you out on the other side with a healthier perspective on living, being and having."

– **Kim Hodous,** The Kitchen Table CEO and best-selling author of *Show Up, Be Bold, Play Big: 33 Strategies for Outrageous Success and Lasting Happiness from a Former Stay-at-Home Mom who Built a 7-Figure Business from her Kitchen Table*

"This book starts off with great thought-provoking questions and then moves on to tips and strategies that are easy to implement. Add the inspiration that is scattered throughout the book and you are there!"

— **Donna Rippley**, Author, *I want a new career, now what do I do?* Founder, www.CenterforCareerTransition.com

"I devoured this highly practical, easy-to-read book, proving it can benefit women and men alike. Barkley offers a simple, step-by-step process that demystifies organizing and demonstrates how 'clutterBusting' is a learnable skill that becomes as innate as reading: once you 'get it,' there's no going back!"

— **Danny Brassell**, "America's Leading Reading Ambassador" www.DannyBrassell.com

" 'MORE LIVING. less stuff'...Isn't that what life is all about? Simple. Profound. Life-changing. Great job, Virginia!"

— **Michelle Prince**, "America's Productivity Coach" www.MichellePrince.com

"ClutterBusting for Busy Women is a thoughtful heartfelt book that touches on the emotional and physical aspects of clutter and helps readers to understand how they are linked."

— **Jewels Muller MA** Chief Chick, www.ChicksConnect.com

"Virginia hits the nail on the head with her evaluation of clutterBusting. It's not about the stuff; it's about our lives. By 'cleaning up' the tangible things, we are empowered to be more fully present and thus more engaged in and excited about the lives we live."

— **Sarah Plummer,** Author, speaker, trainer, advocate www.SemperSarah.com

"If you want to stop feeling like a victim of your crowded closets, crammed cupboards and disheveled rooms, follow Virginia's advice. Victory over clutter will liberate your life!"

– **Jill Hendrickson,** Author, *Victim To Victory: 50 Ways To Overcome Challenges, Reclaim Your Power, And ReCreate Your Life*

"Wow, Virginia gets it! This book is a must-read for anyone that wants to release their energy and creativity. Sharing her knowledge and tools to clear clutter, she takes you step-by-step to create both a peaceful and fulfilled environment. I highly recommend Virginia's book to anyone who wants to clear clutter once and for all and embrace the life you've always dreamed of!"

– **Gary Barnes,** The Traction Coach
www.GaryBarnesInternational.com

"Virginia Barkley has written a masterpiece! She has analyzed in depth the causes for our cluttered lives, and detailed in exquisite prose how to reorganize our very existence. A must-read, several times, and inwardly digest and implement."

– **Marishka Glynne,** Intuitive Consultant and author of *The Master Switch; The Five Steps To Turn On Your Intuition And Turn Up Your Success*

To Life Lived Passionately
& On Purpose!

♡ VA

CLUTTER
BUSTING
for BUSY WOMEN

How To Create A C.A.L.M. Life To Have More Time & Energy

Virginia Barkley

The Organizing Authority

Contents

CONSOLIDATE
PART ONE - THE FIRST PIECE OF THE PUZZLE

ALIGN
PART TWO - THE SECOND PIECE OF THE PUZZLE

LIBERATE
PART THREE - THE THIRD PIECE OF THE PUZZLE

MAINTAIN
PART FOUR - THE FINAL PIECE OF THE PUZZLE

Ode to clutterBusting

I will remember Rome was not built in a day,
and neither was this clutter;

With April showers come flowers in May,
only sunny words to myself I will utter.

While fear and doubt may put me to the test,
to myself I will remain true;

My home is my nest, the showplace of my best,
now enjoying the C.A.L.M. of restored spaces anew.

— Virginia Barkley

Thank You Bonus

I want you to get the maximum benefit from this book. To help you do just that, I've provided a **free audio download** of Chapter One, *Demystifying Clutter*. Visit my website, www.ClutterBustingForBusyWomen.com, and download your **free** mp3 to jumpstart your experience.

To your success!

Dedication

This book is dedicated to my earth angels,
My Family,
and to my guardian angels
who have believed in me, supported me,
encouraged me and cheered for me.
It is in both good times and challenging times
that we are given the opportunity to grow.
I am eternally grateful for all of my life experiences with
you.
To My Devoted Parents,
Constance and Bucky
and
My Sisters,
Charlotte and Constance,

In Memory
of my precious grandmother, Grans,
who chose to live each day of her life gracefully,
in spite of all circumstances,
and model, for me, perseverance beyond measure.

I love you all!

A Letter to My Readers

**We are creating pages of our
personal history each day by
how we choose to live in these
precious, present moments.**

— Virginia Barkley

It's not how much information to which we're exposed that counts. What counts is how we apply that information in our lives to manifest the results we set out to achieve. I challenge you to apply the information I've shared in this book by implementing these clutterBusting activities immediately. I invite you to share your success stories with me!

Before moving back to my native New Orleans in fall 2003, I'd been away from the city for 20 years. I was 40 at the time, renovating a home, and looking forward to settling down with a man I'd been dating long distance for a year.

As fate would have it, Hurricane Katrina struck less than two years later. The city was devastated, my relationship imploded, and I was unemployed. No one from New Orleans escaped emotionally unscathed by the disastrous flood that followed the hurricane. It was a frightening time. We cannot underestimate the toll that trauma takes on our confidence to feel capable of keeping up with the stuff of life. Fear can either inhibit or motivate us when we are faced with adversity.

If I had retreated into what my life had temporarily become and focused on the illusion of the negative situation surrounding me, I'm not sure where I'd be right now. Instead, I decided to use the Katrina experience as a pivot point, and I set about to determine what my next life step would be. I asked myself then what I am requesting you to ask yourself now, "How will I make this situation work for me?"

One way to approach the fear is to respond to it with fun. Whenever a perceived challenging situation presents itself in my life, I like to focus on one of my favorite childhood heroines, Mary Poppins, who said, "With every job that must be done, there is an element of fun; you find the fun and snap the job's a game."

Six months later, I incorporated my business, *Let's Get It Straight LLC*. I hung out my shingle and started helping others by supporting their organizing goals. Seven years later, I am writing, speaking, coaching, and helping more people than I ever dreamed I could reach when I sat on my front porch, in the midst of post-Katrina uncertainty, listening to the nothingness of an abandoned city.

I find that most people interpret uncertainty as a negative word. Yet, if we each look at our lives and reflect on those times of uncertainty, I bet there are more positive outcomes that round out the ends of our stories. **What doors of possibility are waiting for you beyond the clutter?**

The first action for you to take to ensure your success is to put yourself in the category of being an organized person: calm, confidant, and capable of handling anything that comes your way. If your calendar is full or you just need some downtime, then you, as an organized person, can decline requests, block time for recreation or regrouping, and ensure that organizing solutions are integrated into your daily routine. It's essential that you give yourself a time frame for accomplishing your clutterBusting goals. Your impending time frame will keep clutterBusting on your radar as a priority.

The Olympic Games illustrate the necessity to commit to and be consistent within a specific time frame to qualify as a competitor. Athletes set their sights on the four-year time frame. Some make it and some don't; those who don't reset their sights on the next Olympic trials. They don't quit just because they missed their initial goal. They persevere and so do we.

I believe that anything is possible, and **all possibilities begin within us**. I already believe in you. Now it's time for you to believe in yourself.

I encourage you, as you read this book, to begin taking action. Statistics show that if people share their goals with at least one other person, they are 90 percent more likely to achieve those goals. Consider enlisting a friend, who is also ready to bust through her clutter, to become your success partner. The experience will be that much more enriching.

Welcome to the clutterBusting club!

Chapter 1

Demystifying Clutter

*"Sweep away the clutter of things
that complicate our lives."*

— Henry David Thoreau,
American author and poet

I am thrilled that you have decided to journey with me to the core of your clutter and emerge on the other side with a new outlook on organizing as a crucial exercise for sustaining your time, energy, and sanity. The most important thing to remember is that the clutter didn't appear overnight. To start clutterBusting, we must choose to stop contributing to it right now.

Have you ever thought about what clutter is?

The first definition of clutter in both the dictionary and the thesaurus is CONFUSION. It comes from the word *clotter* [to clot], influenced by *cluster* and *clatter*, *hard objects striking against each other in noisy disorder.*

We give words and things and experiences meaning. Our interpretation of those words, things, and experiences can give them power over us...or not. Clutter does not just happen. It's not bigger than we are unless we allow it to be.

Einstein proved that everything is energy. Thus, the stuff in our lives, which manifests itself in paper piles and mess mounds, is just a mass of stuck energy, stuck decisions, objects striking against each other in confusion, constantly reminding us that something in our lives is stuck.

The flip side is that clutterBusting creates this ripple effect in its wake, renewing our energy, increasing our productivity and boosting confidence in our capabilities. The result is a more positive outlook on life overall when that unstuck energy is flowing freely and life resumes a pleasant rhythm.

Contrary to popular belief, **organizing IS a learnable skill**. Most activities in life are achievable if we put our focus and attention on mastering them, or at least learning the basics. Imagine opening a book without having the skill of being able to read; wouldn't that be frustrating? Is reading an innate gift? No! We had to learn how to read. But now, isn't it so natural to you as to feel innate? Yes! And why might that be? Because we have been reading for so long. I have been honing my organizing skills my entire life! **Today is the first day of the rest of your clutterBusting life!**

Organizing is different from cleaning. This mis-understanding is a key factor in the accumulation of clutter. Organizing is not just about following tips to streamline your closet, weed through your papers, or keep dishes out of the sink. While all those tips are beneficial for staying organized, and I integrate them into my organizing practice, they do not encompass what *being* organized means.

Have you ever started working in one area of your home, and while getting it organized, items seem to end up cluttering another area? According to the dictionary, to *organize* is *to arrange into a structured whole*, so it is imperative to look at our environment as interlocking pieces of a jigsaw puzzle. I use the word *environment* loosely, as it includes your home as well as your activities. Clutter manifests itself not only as mess around our homes but also calendar chaos when every moment of our waking hours is booked. Then comes that telling word: *overwhelm*, which means *to cover or bury completely.* What challenge or difficulty might be buried beneath the clutter?

When putting a jigsaw puzzle together, we arrange jumbled pieces into a structured whole. Just as puzzles have borders, so do our homes. Boundaries are a good thing! They help us make decisions and keep our lives in check. Children constantly test boundaries by pushing their parents until their parents draw the line. They subconsciously need to see a line drawn in the sand, and we must also be responsible adults to ourselves and draw the line.

I have an extremely low tolerance for clutter so my line gets drawn quickly. Think about areas in your life where you do draw the line -- in what you like and dislike, what you will tolerate and what you won't. The irony of women being such amazing caregivers is our belief that there is always something more important to take care of than ourselves. It's time to draw the line.

Without structure, clutter sprawls and invades other areas of our lives energetically. Ninety percent of Americans say disorganization at home and at work negatively affects their lives. Eighty-five percent of couples say they argue over clutter and disorganization. These percentages speak loud and clear.

Clutter in households is an equal-opportunity thief stealing the time and energy of all those who live in the home.

Clutter is like a parasite, leaching energy from its host: YOU! It cannot live without you but you CAN live without it. No matter how much we try, we cannot outrun our challenges. We must acknowledge them, acknowledge our feelings about them, and take action to move the energy through us instead of holding onto it, swallowing it, or pretending it's not there.

No one is immune from challenges. How are you currently facing challenges or difficulties in your life?

A) **BOXING GLOVES**: We push the challenge away as if it doesn't belong to us.

B) **DRAMA CLUB**: While the challenge remains on the sidelines we dive into and project our emotions onto every other experience we have as a way to release the energy of pent up feelings.

C) **OFF TO THE RACES**: With our blinders on, we forge ahead as we try to outrun the challenge and leave it behind.

OR.....

GARDEN PARTY: We pull up the weeds, till the soil, replant, fertilize, and water.

A, B, and C are scenarios that most likely result in some form of clutter. **ClutterBusting is your invitation to the garden party.**

ClutterBusting is not an activity done in fits and spurts. It's a project that you commit to, move through and complete, so that you can focus on MORE LIVING with less stuff. As a member of the National Association of Professional Organizers, my intent is to share my strategies that will enable you to ClutterBust your home and maintain the nurturing environment you've created for yourself. ClutterBusting puts you on the path to a healthier lifestyle.

Commitment + Consistency + Time Limit
= Clarity + Calm

All goals worth reaching involve time and focus. If you're serious about clutterBusting, then this activity has to:

1. Join the ranks of other goals you want to achieve;
2. Have a time limit by which you track your progress and make adjustments;
3. Become as habitual as brushing your teeth.

I challenge you to put yourself under a positive kind of pressure to clear the clutter and get on with the more precious activities of life. Pressure creates diamonds and purifies gold. Pressure forces us to test the limits of our perceived capacities. Pressure precedes action.

Doesn't the clutter cause pressure already? Take your pick. If you start strong out of the gates, make headway and then quit halfway through, you still have clutter. And, it could get worse. It's the same as not taking your full prescription of antibiotics because after two doses you feel much better. When you stop taking an antibiotic mid-treatment, your body builds up an immunity which makes it harder for the next regimen of antibiotics to do their work. If you attack your clutter and then back off, you feel more overwhelmed the next time you want to tackle it because you've got that much more to tackle. Stick with it and stick with me to see your CALM dreams come true.

Einstein said, "Nothing happens until something moves," so let's get moving. To your success! I believe in YOU!

Summary Points

- Clutter is stuck energy and provides us with a visual cue that something in our lives is stuck.

- ClutterBusting unsticks the energy resulting in more time and energy to devote to more fulfilling life activities.

- All goals worth achieving involve time and focus.

Chapter 2

Getting Your Brain in Gear

> "One important key to success is
> self-confidence. An important key
> to self-confidence is preparation."
>
> — Arthur Ashe,
>   Professional U.S. tennis player

Any successful journey requires some degree of preparation. We trust the map makers and follow their directions. Similarly, we believe that we'll see the same picture on the jigsaw puzzle box once all the pieces are arranged in the right place.

When beginning a partnership with a new client, I like to first assess the clutter spots that moved them to pick up the phone and call me. I then walk through their entire home assessing room arrangements and closet space because I think of houses as jigsaw puzzles.

When you assess your home space in its totality, and have an overall placement plan for items (versus moving from clutter spot to clutter spot), you will prevent experiencing the scenario I touched on earlier regarding the frustration of cleaning one area by moving the clutter to another area.

My initial assessments include an action plan which I refer to as our roadmap. My clients can then choose to follow my roads, take others, or do a bit of both. You have the opportunity to do the same as I unveil the process for successful clutterBusting.

My clutterBusting puzzle looks like this:

C	Consolidate	Thoughts and Things	T
A	Align	Ideas with Items	I
L	Liberate	Mindset from Material Possessions	M
M	Maintain	Energy and Environment	E

_____ * _____

MORE LIVING. less stuff

Before going any further, you must fully own the belief that **you are capable of busting through your clutter, living life to the fullest, and in an organized fashion,** by first ridding yourself of any unsupportive thoughts that are contrary to this belief.

We must allow ourselves to believe we are worthy and capable of creating a calmer environment in which to live. Time is our most precious commodity and the only thing we can truly count on is this present moment.

The time is now for you to be savoring each day; honoring yourself, your home and its belongings; and endeavoring to enjoy all of life's moments, knowing that when you return to your nest, it will be a place of peace, relaxation, and rejuvenation.

Summary Points

- Before beginning any project, we must get grounded in where we are and where we want to go.

- We must trust in our capabilities and persevere to reach our project destinations.

- The only guaranteed time we have to make changes in our environment is now.

Activity

Take a moment to answer the following questions. This will help you to see on paper where you are versus where you want to be. The chapters that follow will move you toward greater calm in your home and your life from this day forward. Before beginning this assessment, I want you to BREATHE. Give yourself a break. Your clutter did not happen in a day; therefore, clutterBusting is not going to happen in a day. David slew a lion and a bear before he killed Goliath. Think about and answer the following questions...

How long have I allowed this clutter to live in my space?

_____

What was going on in my life when the piles started building?

_____

Most of my clutter accumulates (in what area of my home)

_____

Clutter makes me feel...

_____

What else makes me feel the same way?

_____

I feel disorganized because...

_____

The top three things that keep me from getting organized are:

1.

_____

2.

_____

3.

_____

_____

What really contributes to the clutter around here is...

_____

I could get more organized if...

_____

I want to get organized because...

_____

WHEN I get organized, I will be able to...

_____

The TOP 3 things I want to learn from *ClutterBusting for Busy Women* are:

1.

_____

2.

_____

3.

_____

This book belongs to:

_____

I'm IN and that which no longer serves me
is on its way out!

_____

Signature

_____

Date

**"Outstanding people have one
thing in common: An Absolute
Sense Of Mission."**

— Zig Ziglar

Consolidate

Part One - The First Piece Of The Puzzle

Chapter 3

Consolidate Your Thoughts

"Organize your thoughts around
your dreams and watch them
come true."

— Anonymous

When beginning to put a jigsaw puzzle together, I find
that it's easier to gather all the border pieces first. Once the
border is constructed, there is literally a frame of reference, a
grounding and immediate feeling of accomplishment before
any of the inside pieces have even found their place. The
next step I take is grouping pieces by color, again giving me

a sense that I am getting closer to my goal without having put the first piece into place within the border. Similar actions are taken as our clutterBusting journey begins with consolidation.

We've got to consolidate our thoughts because thoughts dictate our actions and results. If not reined in, our thoughts can derail our best intentions. Along with consolidating them, we must be relentless in our focus on repeating only those thoughts that support us. When thoughts pop up that sabotage our ability to act, we need to turn the volume down. Better yet, just say, "Mute." **The most important six inches in which we start to bust clutter is the space between our ears.**

While well meaning, our ego unwittingly tries to talk us out of trying things, as a means of protecting us from failure. Our ego doesn't want us to put out any energy that may not result in achieving the goals we set out to achieve; it believes that trying is too risky without assurance of success. Ironically, by not trying, we are feeding the belief that we are a failure. By not trying new things, we potentially hold ourselves back and possibly make life more difficult than necessary.

Our formative years were about nothing but trying new thing after new thing, learning and growing with reckless abandon. Yet, as adults, these thoughts of fear and doubt tell us we can't do it, we don't have time, we're fated to be challenged by the clutter in our lives, in our homes, and on our calendars.

A primary reason for getting easily distracted when we want to ClutterBust an area of our homes or offices is that we have multiple thoughts vying for our attention. If we have no goal other than, "I just want this X organized," then any thought that moves us to feel like we're doing something will cause us to switch gears. At the end of the day, we wonder why we're on a different track than we started on that morning.

My initial question to clients is asking them what their vision is for a particular space because that *compelling* vision is what drives us to see results. Your vision has to evoke your interest in a *powerfully irresistible way* as if there is no other option but to see it through to fruition.

What did you dream of being when you were young? It seems that this is the first memory we lose as adults. Imagination and possibility do not have age limits. Nothing keeps children from their imagination, so what happens when those children inhabit larger birthday suits?

Think of Walt Disney, Oprah Winfrey, or J.K. Rowling. All of these people dared to dive into uncharted waters because their compelling visions overpowered their fear. Their thoughts were focused solely on the vision of their success, what it looked like and what they needed to do to make it happen.

The truth of the matter is that not challenging fear keeps us stuck and prevents us from evolving into the perfectly capable people we are born to be. The good news is that where there is fear, there is power. Power comes from the ability to act in spite of fear, taking one step forward again and again. Fearful or doubtful thoughts alone cannot keep us from taking action unless we choose to believe them. Every choice is an opportunity to exercise our power, boost our confidence, and take another step. **The distance between fear and confidence is just one step.**

John F. Kennedy, Jr. is one of the most exceptional examples I know of being open to a compelling vision beyond most men's dreams at the time. He declared to America and the world that we would be going to the moon within a decade after hearing, only the day before from NASA, that it would take a minimum of 40 years!

A big mistake that people make when forging into their clutter is that they don't have a compelling reason to finish and they get distracted easily.

Take for example this scenario....

I decide one morning that I am going to tackle the pile of papers that has accumulated on my desk and has started to sprawl like kudzu. I don't have a functioning filing system and have not thought about where these papers will go once I go through them, but I'm feeling armed with a strong will to dive in and cross this off my list...

I'm about ten minutes into the pile, which has become a new pile of 'papers gone through,' and I discover the itinerary of a trip I took a few months ago. Immediately my thoughts are back in the countryside with friends ... and I realize I never put the pictures in a photo album and maybe that would be a better use of my time....

I abandon the paper pile and refocus on getting those pictures into the album I recently bought. I am a few photos into this new activity when I come across a picture of a wonderful evening out to dinner with friends. As I study the picture, my mind relives the night. The conversation was flowing, laughter in excess, and I realize that I haven't seen that dress I was wearing in the photo since the trip, and I'd really like to wear it to an upcoming party.

Thinking it will only take a minute to check my closet, I abandon the photos and head to my bedroom. On the way, I notice my coffee cup in the den and decide to quickly bring it to the kitchen. While in the kitchen, I suddenly feel hungry. I decide to fix a quick snack and realize that my favorite show is coming on shortly and what can I really get done in that short time frame. Following the show, I make a couple of phone calls, one thing leads to another, and ...

Before I know it, I'm back in the kitchen fixing dinner and the papers are more scattered than they were in the morning, the photos are now sprawled out on the guest room bed, I still haven't found my dress and the day is fast approaching night. No wonder it's hard to get started when you fear that you're going to end the day with a bigger mess on your hands.

Been there? Done that?

Instead of taking a giant leap into the mess with our eyes closed and giving in to distraction, visualizing is about taking one step back and grounding ourselves in the bigger picture before we get started. Then, we are better prepared to take unlimited steps forward once we begin. Doesn't that make more sense? Rather than taking "one step forward and two steps back," my recommendation is to take one step back and two steps forward. In the latter scenario, you'll always be one step ahead!

One of the most famous speeches in history is, "I Have A Dream" and look what happened! Martin Luther King, Jr. spoke in detail as if he could see what was to be the future of our country. Through his eloquent imagery, he engaged all of our senses and pulled us in to grasp the future of his dream.

I want you to consider and to focus on what's in it for you on the other side because that compelling vision will keep you *on track* versus sidetracked. What do you suppose keeps Olympic athletes on track when they're having a tough training day? Every time they practice, Olympic athletes visualize their win.

The result *must* be worth more than the perceived struggle of the effort. Think about learning to ride a bike, swim or, heck, just walk; the focus on the goal of achieving those things kept us going, falling down and getting up, until we got the results on which we had set our sights.

In 2004, I bought a house that needed a complete facelift. I bought this house because it was what I could afford, but the distance between my vision and the disaster that it was seemed enormous. The first action I took was creating a vision book, which included colors, fixtures, flooring, and beautiful spaces that inspired me. My vision book gave me a framework for the project and helped dictate my decisions about certain features in the home, and how I needed to prioritize my time to complete the project.

It makes complete sense that clutter has accumulated if you don't have another vision to replace it. The only way to know what you like and what you don't like is to compare pictures, disqualifying those that don't resonate with you and relishing in the ones that do. The beauty of using magazine pictures is that you're not starting from scratch. You let other people's ideas inspire you, which expands your ability to see the full potential of your spaces, and quite possibly, your life. Bring play and excitement into your organizing efforts. Isn't it exciting to think about living in a calmer and more functional environment? Do you think of your home as your ally or an albatross? Your vision is critical.

Your vision can be in words or pictures (either way, *be specific*). Include all of your senses in your description. It's important not only to see what you want, but to experience the feelings of greater peace and refreshing energy. Close your eyes and imagine yourself in the area you want to clutterBust. What does your newly organized space look like? How does it make you feel? What are you doing in the space? Are you finding things more easily and quickly? Can you now park your car in your garage? What will you do with that extra money once you've let go of the additional storage unit you've been paying for?

Whether you already have your compelling vision, or are just beginning to formulate it, magazine pictures will bring to life your dream spaces and a new vision for CALM living. Create a vision board with these pictures, similar to the one that I am holding up in the picture at the end of this chapter. You can listen to the whole WWL-TV segment on my website.

Taking the time to visualize creates a powerful intention, moving you toward greater clarity and focus on what you want. It also creates tension between the current disorganization and the calmness of what you see every day on your vision board. It is a constant reminder of the disparity between what you have (clutter) and what you deserve (CALM).

CB Tip

Your compelling vision is what you want to see on the box cover for your home's jigsaw puzzle. If you have no idea what you want, then start flipping through magazines and deciding what you like and what you don't like.

Since 85 percent of the papers we file are never looked at again, display your vision board somewhere in your home so that you enjoy it daily and begin to see that you do have a choice. Place your vision board at the entrance of the room you're reorganizing, or put it in your bathroom or kitchen, in a spot where you're sure to consistently notice it. As a busy woman on the go, you can buy an insulated cup that allows you to insert pictures, and then you'll have your vision with you all the time!

When you focus every day on the fact that **you do have an option**, you are more apt to be moved to action because your subconscious will prefer your compelling vision over the current disorder, and it will be constantly saying to you, "I want that!" The vision wall I now have in my office keeps me focused on my intended results, both personally and professionally. It grounds me in what I want for myself, what I need to do and learn to reach my goals, and reminds me daily of why I want to achieve those goals.

Neale Donald Walsch, an American author born in 1943, said, "*Life begins at the end of your comfort zone.*" If you really want to get organized, you have to allow yourself to be discontented with the clutter and to break free from a state of complacency with your current situation. Visualization will reinforce your desire for change. Action toward your desired goals will produce change.

What I've found in my business is that while people may genuinely want to make changes, they don't allow themselves the time or patience to think about how to transition. We waste more time trying to figure out "what to do next" than we would if we invested the time to consolidate our thoughts into a compelling vision that will then dictate the priorities of our project.

Think about a time frame within which you'd like to finish your project. Throughout the process, check in with yourself to see if you've overestimated or underestimated how much time it's taking you. Then, give yourself permission to regroup. It's essential to specify time on your calendar for your organizing project so that it remains a priority. The pressure that we put on ourselves to either do things perfectly or not at all is that protection mechanism that keeps us from trying, completely undermining our own capabilities.

If we were to take the example of planning a vacation, we wouldn't wait until the first day of that vacation to make plans. So why is scheduling our daily life any different? Eventually, we will all run out of days; each one of them not only matters but influences all the days that follow.

Just as it is when putting a jigsaw puzzle together, the picture is only the beginning, but you must have the picture. It becomes your customized destination. It's time to visualize the possibilities. Repeatedly, I have watched organizing dreams manifest into "living" rooms.

Are you familiar with the phrase, "Are we there yet?" When you start hearing that phrase between your ears, just acknowledge it by saying, "Yes!" because where you are is exactly where you're supposed to be. Trust the process and remain true to yourself and your goals.

CB Tip:

It doesn't matter whether you're clutterBusting your home, your office, your calendar or your life-in-general, you must **give yourself time to think about what it is you want in each of those areas, and then schedule time to get things done.** If we don't schedule specific time for activities like clutterBusting, some other activity is going to fill the slot.

The season is always ripe to harvest your imagination.

Summary Points

- ClutterBusting begins with the consolidation of our thoughts into a compelling vision for calm and clutter-free spaces.

- Our compelling vision will keep us focused on our clutterBusting goals.

- It's critical to look at our vision daily to remind ourselves of the organized destination waiting for us at the end of our journey. Your vision is what you see through your windshield. The clutter is what you're leaving behind as you glance to see it getting smaller in your rearview mirror.

Activity

Choose one space in your home that you'd like to ClutterBust as you read through this book. Step One is to create a vision board for that space, bringing to life the destination that you'll be moving toward throughout the process.

Pretend this is a craft project. Turn on some music and sit down with your favorite beverage, your magazines, a piece of poster board (cut in half or one fourth), and VISUALIZE the possibilities. Flip through the magazines, tearing out pictures, words, colors, or anything else that jumps out at you. Refrain from censoring. Just play. You will be amazed at what you create. Have fun!

To watch the TV spot in its entirety, go to
www.ClutterBustingForBusyWomen.com

"Give thanks for what you are now, and keep fighting for what you want to be tomorrow."

— Fernanda Miramontes-Landeros

Chapter 4

Consolidate Your Things

*"The person who moves a mountain
begins by carrying small stones."*

— Chinese Proverb

As children, some of the first skills we learn are putting like with like; identifying which object doesn't belong; becoming aware of sizes, shapes and colors, and discovering that square pegs don't fit into round holes. It is the same with puzzle pieces that look similar to each other when coming out of the box, but are actually separate and distinct.

I'd like you to take a walk through your home, meandering through its rooms. Are there items that you really like but haven't noticed in a while? It might be a painting in the living room or a framed picture in the den. Perhaps it's an object that is displayed on a mantle or dresser. We all have things in our homes that we like; yet, over time and without conscious effort they seem to disappear from our view.

I call this condition **conscious blindness**: when some event, or events, distract us to the point that we fall out of touch with ourselves and our surroundings. It could be an unexpected event or a big life change, or it could just be that we're juggling too many things. Paper piles and mess mounds can't talk back, and, therefore, are easily neglected. Our *figure-ground perception* is compromised.

Figure-ground perception is simply *the ability to separate elements based on contrast*. For example, if an object has remained in the same place for an extended period, its perceived contrast to its surroundings diminishes. This apparent loss of recognition plays a large role in the growth of clutter.

Have you ever looked at a pile and said, "How did it get so large?" Perhaps you weren't even aware of how large it had become until someone stopped by and you suddenly saw the pile through your guest's eyes? Instead of seeing individual things, we just see a big blob of something because we have attempted to tune out the clutter. Unfortunately, our subconscious continues to be plagued and exhausted by the sight of it. Our subconscious is a meticulous observer, working 24/7 and cataloguing all that is happening around us.

The first step in consolidating things is to allow yourself to see the items that are creating the clutter. Really *see* them. To see them, we need to be fully present in the moment and allow our eyes to relax and take everything in without judgment. Just see. I compare this part of the process to a stereogram. A stereogram is an image that when first viewed looks one dimensional; yet, when you put your full attention on it, relax your eyes, and trust, a three dimensional picture emerges.

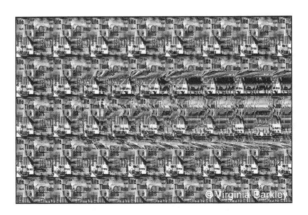

**Can you see what's waiting for you
on the other side of the clutter?**

CB Tip

One of the best ways to stay organized is to have people over more often. I love inviting friends to informal dinners during the week. Even as an organizer, I notice items that need to be put away when I am having company. This exercise engages our awareness muscle. When I was growing up, my mother would clean the house top to bottom before we left for vacation. Along with having someone come check on the pets, my mother wanted the house to be in order when we arrived home after a relaxing trip. Every once in a while, wake up and pretend that you are a guest in your own house and see what things stand out to you.

Typically, when I am helping clients clutterBust, there are multiple categories of items that have gotten jumbled together, creating confusion and the perception of a larger mess. Putting papers with papers, books with books, presents with presents, clothes with clothes and so on, you can significantly consolidate your things. Additionally, the beauty of consolidating clutter by categorizing is that it will give you instant gratification when you see your clutter shrinking.

CB Tip

When people ask me where to start organizing if several spaces have become cluttered, I recommend either the master closet or the kitchen because typically these are the two areas we visit first thing in the morning. What we see, as well as what our subconscious is taking note of, can dictate the quality of our day. **Seeing and feeling calm breeds being calm**.

Do yourself a huge favor and cut down on clutter by immediately avoiding putting anything in bags or totes. Items get lost in bags. Bags crinkle up, mush down, and become less and less attractive to approach because they look tired before we open them again. If you don't know what's in a bag, do you just pull out another so that things don't get mixed up? The paradox is that you then end up with two bags and no idea what's hiding inside them.

Pamela hired me to get her upstairs den organized. When I arrived, I could hardly see the floor. There was a sofa in the room that had become more of a holding deck for boxes, and the *"I don't know what to do with this item"* items. After only one day of simply consolidating items into categories, we ended up sitting on the sofa as my client looked around in amazement at how much more manageable the space looked.

CB Tip

By grouping like items together into categories, we eliminate the negative space around and between objects. You will be shocked at how such a small activity can instantly consolidate your things by a third to a half. It is amazing how much clutter is composed of miscellaneous paper, receipts, empty bags, and trash that can be pitched or recycled.

Consolidation via categorizing also makes it easier to sort through similar items later. For the moment, hold off on trying to answer questions like, "Am I going to keep this?" and, "If so, where am I going to put it?" It is exhausting to be making decisions about items out of context and jumping back and forth from a book, to an item of clothing, to a magazine. Instead, focus on categories. As the Chinese proverb advises, we need to move "small stones" first.

CB Tip

Categorizing takes the concept of the silverware drawer and replicates it for all categories of items. Just as knives, forks, and spoons each have their place, so should every item in your house. Not just almost every item. Every item. If you're starting with your closet, remove all the empty hangers. Put items into categories—blouses, skirts, pants, dresses. Then, take it a step further, and put blouses into categories: sleeveless, short sleeve, long sleeve. Finally, organize your categories by color to create a calmer atmosphere.

It will also make a big difference if you hang your shorter items closer to the door, with a story of shorter to longer unfolding as you walk into the closet. If your closet is not a walk-in, modify this idea to have clothes hung shorter to longer, from left to right. Think about how retail stores display their clothing, by item and color, making it more visually appealing to shoppers.

Once items are categorized, your brain is able to focus on one item grouping, like books. When you can see how many books you have in all, you will be better prepared to make more confident decisions about which ones you want to keep and which ones you can give away. **There is a fine line between keeping items and being kept by them.**

CB Tip

When streamlining books, especially in situations where they are overflowing from bookshelves or you have a storage unit full of them, I counsel my clients to set a goal of letting go of one out of four. I heard this from Peter Walsh, Oprah's organizer. If this sounds radical to you, just remember that $1/4 = 2/8 = 3/12 = 4/16$. Doesn't it sound easier to think that you have to let go of only four out of every 16 books?

In addition, categorizing items allows you to identify multiples of things you have. Often times, we end up buying the same thing several times because we can't find it when we need it; hence, the importance of having a specific place for items.

I have created several in-home office supply areas for clients who have bought, several times over, their organizing supplies because they misplaced the ones they'd previously brought home. I will cover this in more detail in a later chapter; for now, I'd like to underscore the importance of finding appropriate space in your home for each category BEFORE you bring in containers, files, or other organizing supplies, to keep those items more organized. **Beware that when not used properly, organizing containers can quickly contribute to your clutter and unwittingly create more disorganization.**

My rule of thumb is to keep like items together so that there is one central location to look for that category (for example: tools, gardening items, vases, office supplies). This saves an immense amount of time when you have to look in only one place. There can be some exceptions to this rule; people typically like to have things like scissors, pens, and flashlights in various places.

CB Tip

If you pick up a pen to write and it's out of ink, throw it away. "Later" is an illusion that never happens. Don't put off until tomorrow what you can do "in the moment" today. Pens are like bunnies in the home. All the socks that go missing seem to return as pens. Pens are a huge category that easily becomes clutter infiltrating several areas of the home.

This is about trusting yourself to remember where the category is stored. It is also about trusting yourself to return the item to its designated space. If this is speaking to you, I want you to ask yourself why you feel the need to have an excessive amount of one item. I'm asking you to think about it because I've had to think about it too.

For example, during a business trip to Czechoslovakia, I found a unique set of handmade mugs that I loved and thought *I had to have*. Can you relate to that feeling? There were six in the store so I bought them. All of them.

During a conversation with my Czechoslovakian colleague, after I'd returned to the states, I asked him if he would mind going back to the store to see if they had replenished their supply of mugs; I thought an even dozen would be ideal. His response gave me pause. He said, "Well, you already have six, yes? How many more do you really need?"

My answer was that I didn't need any of them and it was in that moment that I learned a valuable lesson about appreciating beauty without having to take a piece of it home with me. I still have those mugs and I alternate among them to make sure each one is used.

This example is also about feeling comfortable and safe. Drinking coffee reminds me of my mother and conjures up feelings of comfort and safety; while no amount of mugs will replace the comfort and safety I felt with my mother, I am able to now provide for myself that comfort and safety, and do so in more fulfilling ways than drinking coffee out of an endless number of mugs.

Of course, the shopping is the fun part, right? However, the endorphin high of the purchase wears off. If you start buying new things without a game plan in place for how they'll be used, I promise that you will end up perpetuating the cluttered situation that you're trying to eliminate.

I was helping Sarah consolidate and categorize belongings after the death of her very organized husband.

In the midst of going through boxes that had been kept in an offsite storage facility for years, I found a misfiled life insurance policy that the couple had forgotten about. She used that money to live on for the following year! You can read the complete article on my website.

It's imperative to consolidate your things. Once items are categorized, and thus consolidated, you'll know how much space you need to store the items as a group—again, putting clothing, entertaining platters, files, games, linens, suitcases, and other such categories, with their buddies!! They want to hang with their buddies! **Like likes like**. If you start putting items away before categorizing them, you'll miss the benefit of consolidation, risk running out of space and resort to splitting up the category, making it more difficult to find things later on.

This is just the second step, so clear your mind of anything but your compelling vision while you put apples with apples, shoes with shoes, totes with totes, and books with books.

Summary Points

- A big reason for the accumulation of clutter is falling out of awareness with our surroundings. I refer to this condition as *conscious blindness*.

- It's necessary to first see the clutter before we can bust through it; seeing it requires us to categorize the contents of its make-up.

- It's easier to bust through clutter when items are consolidated into categories.

Activity

Practice categorizing the items in your purse or in the kitchen catchall drawer to get the hang of consolidating items into categories. Then move on to the area that you chose to work on while reading this book. With your vision board close at hand, categorize the items that are creating the clutter and witness the wonder of consolidation.

Align

Part Two - The Second Piece Of The Puzzle

Chapter 5

Align Your Ideas
With Your Items

"All the art of living lies in a fine
mingling of letting go and holding on."
— Havelock Ellis,
British psychologist/writer

Now that you have consolidated your thoughts, by creating
your compelling vision for your space or spaces that need
clutterBusting, *and* you've consolidated your things into
categories of items, it's time to align the two.

Home is our nest, our place of refuge, satisfaction and refueling. Most of our days begin and end at home. No matter what we do to create moments of relaxation and enjoyment during the day—lunch with friends, a great workout or a manicure/pedicure—we're met with reality when we step through our home's front door. Whether we're met by clutter or calm will either negate or reinforce those moments of relaxation and enjoyment we've recently experienced.

So, why doesn't organizing take center stage? I believe it goes back to our interpretation of words. I believe the word "organize" has gotten a bad rap. Frankly, it sounds like work as much as "vacation" sounds like play. Wouldn't it be easier to say, "Today, I am going to play with my things!" The clutter IS made up of your things, so if you don't want to look through it, or you're spending more time away from home in order not to deal with it, doesn't that tell you something?

In China, one of the oldest civilizations in the world, the Chinese believe that the way spaces are arranged, as well as the objects that inhabit those spaces, can literally dictate the level of health, well-being and good fortune we experience in our lives. I'd like you to take a moment and think about what is literally hanging over your head, day in

MORE LIVING
less stuff

and day out, in your attic. Or, are there any packed closets or drawers leaching energy from rooms? Energetically, clutter is weighing you down, regardless of whether you're consciously thinking about it.

The television show, "Hoarders," examines the impact of clutter, in its extreme form, on individuals and their families. These extreme situations depict an exaggeration of the belief that belongings can somehow replace feelings or experiences, which obviously is not the case because more and more stuff keeps coming into the home.

All of our thoughts, feelings, and actions are born out of our personal beliefs of the world and the role we play in it. Trauma, loss, and sadness when not acknowledged can lead one into a state of paralysis. **It is an illusion to believe that some *thing* will remove the pain or be the cure.** Yet, it's easier to believe in "the thing" because it is tangible; we can hold it and personify it. We need to acknowledge the feelings associated with whatever void a negative experience has caused, or clutter can potentially become the manifestation of those feelings, saying, "look at me."

Sometimes, it's those very things we buy when we're low that bring us down years later because they remind us of a difficult time. In other cases, we punish ourselves by keeping items to remind us of the pain, or to humble us in our guilt

57

about an experience or situation that we can't now go back and change. Obligation to others is yet another excuse we use to tie ourselves down with items that add to our clutter.

One of my clients, Laura, was holding on to a lamp she'd bought with money her father had given her. She liked the lamp because it reminded her of her father, who had passed away more than 20 years prior. It was in good condition, but she had no place to use it. Not using it made her feel guilty but she couldn't part with it. The idea of keeping it or letting it go caused the same feelings, which meant the feelings would be there with or without the lamp. Can you see the invisible layers of clutter piled on top of this item?

Since the lamp was attractive and worked, it could be beneficial to someone else. I asked her if her father would rather have someone use it or see it stored in a closet for another 20 years. She chose the former. Then I asked her how it would feel to donate it with the knowledge that both she and her father would be helping someone else. Instead of feeling guilty and unappreciative for giving it away, she changed her perspective and felt generous for helping someone else.

Holding on to mementos of great experiences can be just as dangerous if those items make us feel like the good old days are gone. Why can't every day be a good old day?

This is your life. This is a new day. If you are living from a place of integrity, and you unwittingly make a mistake or hurt someone's feelings, so be it. You make amends as best you can and carry on. If you are afraid of hurting the feelings of someone who has passed through this world, then rethink whether you are living in the present or the past. This piece of the puzzle focuses on the importance of being in alignment with ourselves rather than always trying to be in alignment with everyone else! Remember, the first definition of clutter = confusion = a breakdown of order = something is out of alignment.

Now that we have our compelling vision, we can begin to look at our items with greater discernment. Prioritizing belongings helps us focus on surrounding ourselves with only those items that lift us up, make us happy, and nourish us in our present lives. These items are in multiple categories including, but not limited to, clothing, furniture, artwork, decorative items or a special inheritance.

Can we agree that we all have items in our houses that we no longer use, haven't used in years, or used to like but have outgrown? Maybe the items no longer suit our tastes.

Organizers have to make hard decisions too. I know first hand how hard it is to let go of things I've cherished in the past but serve no purpose in my present life and are taking up valuable space and energy in my home. At 5 foot 4 inches, I played volleyball in high school. It took a lot of hard work and energy for me to not only be on the team, but to be a starting player.

I was ecstatic my senior year when we won the state championship. I definitely count it as a highlight in my life. Yet, a few years ago, I realized that I didn't need my letter sweater to elicit feelings of the win, especially because I didn't find myself going back to look at it. It was just there, hanging year after year in my closet being ignored. After twelve years of only giving it attention when I needed to pack it up and move it, again, I decided to let it go.

CB Tip

Consider taking a picture of sentimental items and putting them in a memory journal, along with the story of why the item meant so much to you. It's much easier to pass down a book to your children than a box of trophies that have been stored in the attic.

I know people who still pull out their letter sweaters, jackets, and even uniforms and wear them from time to time which is great. I, on the other hand, was doing nothing with mine. A few have asked me on occasion if I regret giving my sweater away.

I find regret to be a very ambiguous word. The root feeling behind regret is sorrow over something that happened ... or didn't happen. If we regret something that didn't happen (i.e., leaving the sweater to hang in the closet indefinitely), is that assuming that we know how the experience would have played out? It's normal to feel sorrow when we let go of anything to which we have an emotional attachment. So, did I have a pang of sorrow? Of course. However, I chose to trust that those wonderful feelings and memories of the win live within me forever, to re-greet the present moment with happiness for having the experience, and to focus on exploring new experiences that will elicit similar euphoric feelings.

We are the sum of our experiences regardless of whether we have a memento from the event sitting on a shelf. Most of those memorable knickknacks that we hold onto are stowed away, or crammed away somewhere, signaling to the universe that we believe it was a once-in-a-lifetime experience that we have to hold onto, rather than appreciating our experiences and finding ways to re-create those feelings. **It's not the experience or the object that we are attached to so much as it is the feelings that that experience elicited.** We have both the capability and capacity to generate those feelings through new (and updated) experiences.

As a native New Orleanian, I am part of a devoted food culture. We place a high value on our dining experiences which can be expensive, but we don't hold on to the food. We savor the tastes of the meal, enjoy the company in that moment, and look forward to the next memorable experience.

Objects are like people; they have a lifespan. We're not required, nor are we obligated to, keep things forever. Remember the meal! Unlike people, objects don't evolve. That's why we continue to buy new things that usually are replacing something that is no longer serving a purpose or suiting our taste.

There are certainly things from my childhood that I have chosen to keep. As Havelock Ellis, the British psychologist and author, says, *"all the art of living lies in a fine mingling of letting go and holding on."* When you are in alignment with yourself, then your choices of what to keep and what to let go will come more easily because you are focused on an outcome greater than any one thing.

When I graduated from college, I moved across the country. I was living in a small apartment with two roommates when my mother started sending me my stuff, and it was stuff. Fortunately, I had no place to store it, so I had to go through it. It did take time for me to sort through everything, but as a young single person with fewer responsibilities, I had more time to go through it than I would now. You are not responsible for holding onto all this stuff. It was my stuff not my mother's. When we have fewer days ahead of us than behind us, we don't want to spend those days wading through other people's clutter, even if it belongs to our beloved children.

We all have enough of our own stuff to weed. I strongly encourage you to take responsibility for your stuff now, rather than pass it on for your children to handle. It takes, on average, seven years to grieve the death of a parent. I have witnessed many times the difficulty that children have had after the death of a parent. To cope with the emotional loss, and have that grief exacerbated by trying to make guilt-free decisions over what to do with the possessions left behind makes the process even more difficult.

Now that you've embraced and recommitted to the organizer in you and given yourself permission to believe in your vision, it's time to gracefully and objectively look at what items have become trapped in the clutter. When getting our thoughts and things aligned, I play a little game to help me and my clients prioritize. We assess belongings, in all categories, as *Friends*, *Strangers*, or *Acquaintances*.

I was introduced to this idea in Judith Kolberg's book, *What Every Professional Organizer Needs To Know About Chronic Disorganization*. This book has great games to play that make organizing more fun regardless of whether you think of yourself as chronically disorganized. While Judith allows her clients to formulate ideas for what *Friend*, *Acquaintance*, or *Stranger* means, I came up with descriptions for each:

Friends are items we use on a daily basis. We notice these *Friends* as we're walking through our home; they define our decorative aesthetic, they are the 20 percent of clothing we wear 80 percent of the time. We know them well.

Acquaintances are items we use occasionally throughout the year. They are those items we keep on hand for travel, entertaining, or decorating for the holidays. We see them occasionally.

Strangers, on the other hand, are items we've forgotten we have. They're loitering in our homes collecting dust. They don't speak to us and we don't speak to them! When my friend Anne's great aunt died, Anne was looking through stuff in the attic and found a box marked: Pictures Of People We Don't Know!

Alignment begins when we start to identify the *Strangers* and let go of them first. Letting go and donating *Strangers* allows you to see how good it feels each time you lighten your load a little, and it boosts your confidence to continue. This stage of clutterBusting is like eating an artichoke. Even if you've never eaten an artichoke, have you seen one? You may be familiar with hearts of artichoke sold in the grocery, the fleshy part of the artichoke found in the center of the vegetable. We have to peel away the smaller outer leaves first with the goal of getting to the heart of our belongings which have been hidden from our view, enjoyment, and appreciation because of the distracting clutter.

ClutterBusting is about modifying home environments to represent who we are today. That includes all environments that make up our home: drawers, closets, basements and attics, along with rooms.

Take a moment and think about a *Stranger* living in your house right now. Also, think about why you still have it or are holding onto it. Typically, clients are able to identify and let go of some of the *Strangers* easily, and yet some of those *Strangers* trip us up.

What I've found in my research and experience is that the deep root that tugs at our decision-making capabilities and creates hesitation to make a decision is uncertainty. Yet, can we ever really be certain of anything other than the very moment we are living in?

The last time I visited my Aunt Deanne, in Hawaii, was a special one. I spent most of my time with my first cousin, Johnny, and his wife and two boys. On the day I was leaving, Johnny, 41, was diagnosed with leukemia. Of all the pictures I took, there was not one with Johnny and me, and I was sick over it. He died three months later. I kept a photograph for years on my dresser of me with his wife and two boys because I knew he was behind the camera. While I loved the picture, it was a constant reminder to me of the one I didn't have. It was then that I finally realized that better than any photo, I had gotten to spend incredible quality time with my cousin and that experience lives in my cells.

My sister shared with me some sage advice years ago. She said, "We make decisions based on the information we have in the moment that we make the decisions. If those decisions are made to the best of our ability, then new information which presents itself later on, is not relevant to our former decision and is best dismissed." It relieves much guilt.

This uncertainty that keeps us from taking the steps necessary to get organized is also the number one reason we hold onto our things long after they've served their purpose. Doubt takes us out of action. We're asking ourselves, "Has this just gotten to be too much to overcome? Can I really do this? Maybe I'm just fated to be disorganized ... yes?" NO! If you believed that, you never would have picked up this book. I don't believe in coincidences. Everything happens FOR us, and this book was written for you! I am certain of only one thing—uncertainty—and I'm OK with that.

The best way to emerge from the fog of uncertainty is to *Just Do Something*, anything, to reinforce your ability to act. Both action and inaction are decisions; if you choose to not do anything, then the unresolved situation—unattended papers, stagnating mail, dirty dishes, clothes that need altering, furniture that needs to be repaired, well-intended projects, an overextended calendar of events—drains more power, time and energy from us.

Taking action moves us out of doubt and puts us back on track to achieve our goals, which could just be to reclaim our energy and zest for life. Any goal is better than no goal. While it may sound counterintuitive, action infuses us with energy to keep getting things accomplished.

Items fall within three primary areas of uncertainty: items that are sentimental, items having real or perceived value, and items we believe we may need in the future. The following questions will help you make your decisions more easily.

Question One: How does the item make you feel? Happy about today or longing over times past? Vibrant and alive or tired and overwhelmed? Obligated to keep it or excited to use it? Does it weigh you down or energize you?

When my friend, Emma, got married, she received a beautiful antique jewelry box as a wedding gift. Two weeks after the wedding, the friend who gave it to her died. While the box was lovely, it was a constant reminder of a dear friend lost. After five years of marriage, she decided to sell it in her garage sale. When a woman inquired about the price, Emma just gave it to her, releasing the energy that had been attached to the item and allowing it to be cherished fully by someone else.

Regardless of sentiment, obligation, or value, if you have something in your house that is eliciting any negative feelings, then I suggest you sell it, give it away or donate it and choose to live in your truth instead of under someone else's influence. We're all adults which means we can give ourselves whatever permission we need to do what's best for us, as long as we are not intentionally hurting anyone. Remember, we are talking about inanimate objects here. The objects don't have feelings.

If you're holding onto something for fear of hurting a friend's feelings, then you need to evaluate the communication you have with that friend. We are not obligated to keep everything that we've been given. Out of respect, we gratefully acknowledge and show our appreciation for others' thoughtfulness to us when we receive a gift. That's all anyone really wants: acknowledgement, appreciation, and kindness.

My father receives gifts, thanks the givers, and usually puts the items back in their boxes where they remain. It used to really bother me, especially because I would ask him what he wanted, give it to him, and he still didn't use it. I then had a simple epiphany: I can't control what he does with what I give him. The joy for me became my ability to find and give him what he asked for, rather than care what he did with it once it was out of my hands.

Question Two: Is it being used?

Think about the last time you used it, or if you have ever used it. What's the worst thing that could happen to you if you let it go? If we acknowledge upfront the possibility of regret, and appreciate it as one of the emotional stages of letting go, then we can acknowledge it for what it is when it rises up to discount our decision. Most importantly, if you're not using it, might it be *immediately* beneficial to someone in need if donated? **Keep in mind that clutterBusting your lifestyle is not only benefiting you, but also benefiting those who are disadvantaged because of their situations.**

When helping my client, Samantha, streamline her clothes, there was a sweater at the bottom of the pile that looked both worn out and neglected. When I asked her if it was a stranger, she said, "Oh no! That's the sweater I was wearing when I met my husband. I don't wear it anymore but I don't think I can part with it." I asked her to consider that since she was now married to this wonderful man and would be with HIM for the rest of her life, perhaps the sweater no longer represented the relationship that she and her husband currently shared. Laughing, she placed the sweater in her donate pile.

Question Three: What would I be doing with my time if I didn't have all this clutter taking time and energy away from more fulfilling pursuits?

My trademark motto is "MORE LIVING. less stuff." Instead of allowing your physical surroundings to leach energy from you, why not clutterBust once and for all, step by step, start to finish. Free up your environment and your calendar to engage in activities that energize you, align with your greater purpose for living, and give you the feeling of having the wind at your back instead of having the proverbial monkey on your back.

Have you experienced laughter yoga? Is there a park nearby where you can walk with friends? When was the last time you went bike riding? Are there any classes offered in your community that sound interesting to you?

Are there dreams that you've let go of because of your age? The essence of life is learning, growing, and expecting dreams to come true. George Weiss, a lifelong tinkerer, came up with a word game, Dabble, when he was 31. In 2011, 53 years later, George found a company to invest in Dabble, which was named Game of the Year in *Creative Child Magazine*!

Could the clutter in your home or on your calendar be a wall that you've subconsciously built around yourself to keep you from doing the things that you love? Has it been there so long that it has become part of how you define yourself, and without it what would you be? When you let go of the clutter, a huge beautiful space in your life opens up to be filled with new experiences, happiness, and greater purpose. The beauty is that all you have to do is let go and press the reset button, reminding yourself everyday as you look at your vision board that the picture in front of you is where you're headed.

Stephen Covey, most well-known for his best seller, *The Seven Habits Of Highly Effective People*, said, "The key is not to prioritize what's on your schedule, but to schedule your priorities." Make the decision and commit to a specific time frame to bust through the clutter in your home or on your calendar, so that you can follow through on key priorities. Start by escorting the *Strangers* out the door first. Then reassess your *Acquaintances* if you're still challenged by space constraints. I advise clients to keep some shelves empty to allow for greater energy flow and open spaces to welcome new opportunities.

While I was speaking, during a television interview, about *Friends*, *Acquaintances*, and *Strangers*, the reporter posed this question to me. "So, Virginia, if your linen closet is overflowing, do you look for a larger space for the category?" What a great question! The answer is a resounding ... NOOOO! You streamline your linen closet first to identify whether there are items that you can give away. Unlike gas and liquids, solid items on their own do not fill every bit of space available. I strongly encourage you to keep space empty in your closets to allow for both you and your things to breathe easier.

My client, Katherine, recently widowed, was downsizing from a 6,000-square-foot home into a 2,500-square-foot-cottage in another state. The home had been her mother-in-law's childhood home, then her husband's childhood home, then the home where Katherine and her husband raised their children. She had an accumulation of almost 80 years of belongings. Together, we assessed what to keep, sell, donate, send to her children, and inventory for her grandchildren. Choosing which items to take with her, and aligning her possessions with how she envisioned her new life, made it easier to decide what to keep and what to leave behind.

Using a floor plan created to scale, I planned the placement for her furniture and redecorated the new space. I worked with movers to pack her up and unpack her so that everything was in its place by the time she arrived: artwork hung, bookshelves arranged, clothing put away, beds made, and food in the refrigerator. When she arrived, she could immediately start living in her new home and cultivating a new chapter in her life. That's what I want for each of you—that you continually assess your lives to ensure that your ideas and items remain in alignment with your lives as they are today.

Since the days on my high school volleyball team, I have been blessed to have great coaches in my life. No matter how much we think we know or how much we think we can accomplish, openness to learning and growing from others is the greatest gift we can give to ourselves. I hope my clients think of me as their success coach.

Whether you embark on the clutterBusting adventure with an organizer, an objective friend, or family members, I encourage you to find a success partner to keep you on track, helping to create peaceful and functional environments from which you can spread your wings daily and fly.

Aligning our thoughts with our things takes the pressure off of us as we bust through our clutter because we are deferring to our greater and more compelling vision to dictate what stays and what goes.

Summary Points

- Clutter can overshadow joyful experiences when it greets you upon your return home, indicating lack of alignment between our external activities and our internal or nesting environment.

- A majority of clutter that has accumulated over years is due to our strong feelings associated with certain items.

- Alignment allows us to defer to our compelling vision or clutter-free destination and to assess items as *Friends*, *Acquaintances*, and *Strangers*, to support our decisions of whether to keep or let go of items.

- For *Strangers* tugging at your heart strings, ask yourself the three questions posed in this chapter.

Activity

Pick up a produce box the next time you're at the grocery and place it in the closet nearest to the front door, or the garage or, better yet, the trunk of your car. For the next week, exercise your awareness muscle and weed out as many *Strangers* as you can. When you identify them, put them in the box. At the end of the week, bring the box to a donation site.

Get in the habit of having a donation box on hand so there is a specific place to put items that are leaving the home. Make sure the box is medium to large in size so that a lot of little donation piles don't become clutter.

During the clutterBusting process, visit your donation site once a week versus waiting to have everything ready to go at once. It's much easier to bring items in phases than to amass a clutter of clutter.

Chapter 6

Localize Your Items With Your Lifestyle

"If a home doesn't make sense, nothing does."

— Henrietta Ripperger,
American writer and author
of a 1948 household manual

With our thoughts and our things now consolidated and aligned, it's time to address whether our things are in the most *sensible* places in our homes. Take note that I did not say rational. Avoid trying to think of where you *should* put something versus where it makes sense in the context of your life and your home. I refer to this strategy as localizing. This stage of alignment is critical in keeping the clutter from returning; it refers to the intuition behind where we choose to localize, or specifically place, our *Friends* and *Acquaintances* while they're not being used.

When you look around your home at where the clutter has accumulated and that clutter is made up of much the same category, then one tack to take is to work with the clutter versus fighting against it. In the area of persistent clutter, consider an organizing solution for that specific area rather than moving items to a place that doesn't feel right. Where possible, create a way to store those items in an organized fashion exactly where they are energetically being drawn. A very simple example is keeping your keys near the door that you use as your primary exit. Does your mail end up in a pile in the same place over and over? Think about placing a basket there to "corral" it, a concept that I will cover in more detail in a later chapter.

Every home has a floor plan. When I bought and renovated my 108-year-old home, I had it gutted. I would go over to the empty structure and walk through it, imagining what I was going to be doing in each room, and where my belongings were going to be placed. No matter how long you have lived in your home, there is no law that says objects must remain in their original place forever. I am a big proponent of moving things around to keep environments fresh and to stimulate our senses, specifically to heighten our awareness of our surroundings.

When you walk through your home and think about what you do in each of the rooms, are the items that you use in the rooms nearby? For example, it wouldn't make much sense to keep the television remote in the foyer if the television is in the den. Are your coffee cups near the coffee maker? Where do you store the coffee?

Women are aesthetic creatures. Beauty relaxes us. When I come home tired after a full day of living, I want to have everything I need within arm's reach. For example, I can sit at my desk, open my mail, shred trash, pay my bills, file my paperwork, check my email, print a document from my computer and make a phone call without ever having to get out of my office chair! My desk looks out onto my front garden, so I have a relaxing view to enjoy while I handle necessary paperwork.

A great visual drill to try is this; if you're in the kitchen and the house catches on fire, do you know exactly where to find the few items you'd want to reach for as you're running out the door? If you live in an area where evacuations for hurricanes, fires, and floods are frequent, this is especially important.

Keep it simple and make the locations work for you. Localization creates a calmer energetic flow throughout the home. Ask yourself, "Where am I likely to look for this" versus "Where should I put this." Your home and its belongings are supposed to support you, so get them in alignment with your lifestyle. Remember, everything is energy. If items are continually finding their way back to a specific location, then that location is obviously a high activity area.

While most people refer to the kitchen as the heart of the home, I refer to it as the stomach because everyone who comes into the home passes through the kitchen, along with everything they're carrying. Mail, school papers, sports equipment, groceries, and much more end up in the kitchen with some things digested more quickly; groceries put away, mail sorted, invitations pinned on a family activity board ... but then some items just sit and sit and sit. **Too much on our proverbial plate is like too much in our stomach— hard to digest**.

Raise your awareness of what those sedentary items are, and look around the space to identify an area where those items can live while they're not being used. Use your judgment to make choices about what is necessary to remain in a certain room based on what activities are most likely to take place there; if the shoe doesn't fit in the living room, then get it out!

The importance of planning the localization of items before anything is put away or relocated ensures that the space you pick can accommodate the whole category. Otherwise, you have similar items in more than one area which defeats the purpose of making it easy for you to quickly and easily find and choose from your entire assortment, of vases, for example.

My home has a large room that includes both the kitchen and den areas. To illustrate localizing for you, I am going to use this room. I have a cabinet next to the back door that is home to my gardening items. There is a table under a window where my kitties hang out, so all of their toys go underneath that table. The entertainment center holds music, movies, magazines and throw blankets for cozy nights on the sofa. My things are physically aligned with my lifestyle.

Being organized is not about being perfect. Nothing and *no thing* will ever be perfect. It does not mean living in a home that could be photographed for a magazine at a moment's notice. It does mean that I can pull my house together daily because I know where everything belongs.

My sticky-note activity keeps me from feeling like I am drowning in a never ending list. Active thoughts stay in sight, and once an item is taken care of, it's fun to remove the note. When organizing is fun, it's a whole new experience.

It's much easier for your eyes to scan notes with one idea on each than to read an endless list that exhausts your brain to look at it. It's hard to celebrate crossing something off your list when you still have seventy-nine other items staring you in the face. Getting three to five concrete things done in a day is better than dabbling in twenty.

I'd like to back up for just a moment to point out that powerful thoughts, insights and new ideas come to us when we are engaged in relaxing activities: showering, cooking, walking. ClutterBusting is important for so many reasons, not the least of which is giving our minds the ability to breathe. The calmer our environment is, the more opportunity for powerful thoughts from our wise mind to get our attention. Aren't you curious to know what powerful thoughts within you are waiting to enrich your life beyond the clutter?

Our homes are composed of "living" rooms. Give yourself permission to move things around. PLAY! I moved my office from the den area to a room in the front of my house because I didn't want to see my paperwork while I was relaxing. It's your home! Keeping things the same as they've always been, hoping for change, and expecting different results is the same as getting up every morning and putting on a straitjacket.

Try moving a few small items into different locations to get used to the way it feels. I know how uncomfortable it may feel initially, but allow yourself to try something new. You can always put things back. When I put my house in Atlanta on the market for sale, my real estate agent requested that I put away all my pictures and any small decorative items. I didn't think a thing about it until I was in the midst of the activity, and I started to feel uncomfortable. All of a sudden, it didn't feel like home, but I stuck to the goal. A few days later, I realized that I felt better about having less stuff around me. Give it a try.

Summary Points

- Localizing is about placing items in locations where you are most likely to be drawn to find them.

- If a certain category of items is always creating clutter in the same place, then create storage in that area when possible.

- Make sure that when you assign a category of items to a certain location, that location can accommodate the whole category.

Activity

Imagine that you are a guest in your own home and see if the placement of items makes sense to you. Take note of how close items are to their point of use.

LIBERATE

PART THREE - THE THIRD PIECE OF THE PUZZLE

Chapter 7

Liberate Your Mindset From Your Materials

"Don't Let Your Clutter Eclipse
The Best Of You."

— Virginia Barkley

Our sense of belongingness is a basic human need that begins at conception; ideally, two people who feel a deep connection and belongingness with one another contribute part of themselves to create the embryo within a mother's womb. We are connected to our mothers for nine months by an umbilical cord, our literal lifeline for survival.

Notwithstanding our need for air, food and water, I believe *belongingness* is the most fundamental of human needs. Our ability to satisfy this sense of belongingness influences us in a variety of ways, one of which is the emotional attachment we project onto inanimate objects.

There are two key considerations of belongingness. One is the depth to which we feel connected to others, including family, friends, colleagues and our community. The other, and arguably more important consideration, is the depth to which we feel connected to ourselves, especially during transitional or challenging times.

Experiences cause feelings. Unacknowledged feelings lead to distraction. Distraction disconnects us from the present moment. When disconnected, we are unable to see what is happening around us and we fall into "conscious blindness." Clutter begins when we let go of a part of ourselves. We either try to fill the void with some *thing* to help us feel better, or we disconnect from our surroundings, which prevents us from being aware of stuff that is piling up.

When we're not in alignment, something's got to give. We pull back and something gets buried, which begins the formation of clutter. To bury something, a pile has to form on top of it. The clutter pile often brings up whatever feelings the experiences first caused. Everything is energy.

The clutter has now taken on the energy of whatever feelings we've tried to distance ourselves from. Clutter can be useful if we use it to get to the root issue that is causing it to grow. We can ask ourselves, "How does this clutter make me feel? Where is that feeling coming from? What do I need to do to release that feeling?"

In my work, I have studied certain words associated with the make-up of clutter, and *belongings* is one such word. We refer to the objects that we have in our homes as belongings, possessions, property, personal effects.

The paradox is that while we feel disconnected from the clutter, the clutter is only a manifestation of a deeper disconnection from others or from ourselves. It is that disconnection that is causing more anxiety than the clutter; however, the clutter allows us to project or displace our anxiety.

Many things create disconnection. Losses of any kind—death, separation, job security, or our homes, for example—create this disconnection. When our activities are running our lives, we can lose our footing. (Did you know that we lose a lot of energy through the bottom of our feet?) This is why alignment with our thoughts is so important.

We must be diligent about checking in with ourselves, accepting where we are, and making sure we stay engaged with others, nurturing our belongingness. Just sharing fears and frustrations with someone immediately releases the negative energy and opens up space for positive change. The biggest part of the fear is the sense of losing our belongingness, either past or present. Yet, by stating our fear, we secure our belongingness, diminish the fear, and are better able to address our present circumstances.

I was devastated when my doctor told me that I had to have a hysterectomy in my early 40's. I couldn't face myself, much less anyone else, with the news that having a child was not in the cards for me. I sent an email to my close friends, not having enough courage to talk about it with anyone. Then, I received a call from one of those friends, Kelly, who had received my email. She urged me to call her because she'd just been diagnosed with breast cancer, and she wanted to talk!

While I was holding onto negative feelings about myself and my circumstance, she was telling friends of her situation, releasing her energy of uncertainty and fear, and being filled with positive nurturing. She was using her circumstances as a means to deepen her belongingness; by expressing her fear, she pulled me out of having to carry mine on my own. **The more we share, the less we bear of fear, insecurity, and clutter.** As Deepak Chopra says, *"My witnessing of my fear will transform it into love."*

The irony of clutter is that while we're burying unaddressed feelings beneath it, it's creating a mess we can't ignore! Clutter is just the symptom. If we approach it as such, and with gratitude for disabling us from going any further without addressing our feelings or needs, we are on the verge of a huge breakthrough. The secret of happiness is expressing gratitude for whatever circumstance we find ourselves in because it is an opportunity for growth.

The next time you feel compelled to buy something you hadn't even gone out to get, ask yourself what it is that you really need, because chances are it has more to do with feeling emotionally connected to and fulfilled in your world. Eventually, the high of the buy wears off; when that happens, we are faced with asking ourselves the questions posed in Chapter Five. Instead of rushing out to invite a *Stranger* in, you might consider reaching out to help someone in need. The act of helping someone else has a more lasting, fulfilling effect than helping yourself to more clutter.

A few years back, I was engaged to be married and the engagement fell through six weeks before the wedding. It was one of the lowest moments of my life. A couple of weeks later, I was going through the motions of fixing breakfast one morning when I heard a petition on the radio for donations to help build a fishing village in Haiti. Instead of just asking for donations, the radio host was saying that for one price you could buy a window or a door.

So I decided to buy a roof! Standing in my kitchen, I bought a roof, and I realized I had turned a corner. I felt alive and was energized by the belongingness of helping others. When we choose to separate our feelings from our belongings (or attachments), we have the opportunity to connect more deeply with ourselves and others.

"Sesame Street" has an activity accompanied by a song that says, "one of these things is not like the other ... one of these things doesn't belong." While there is no way for me to see what kinds of things are contributing to your clutter, I can tell you with certainty that the one thing that absolutely does not belong in the middle of it is you!

Summary Points

- Our sense of belongingness, or connection, is a key factor in the accumulation and dissipation of clutter.

- No matter how many things we choose to add to our surroundings, those things are inanimate objects incapable of replacing our need for belongingness and human connection.

- Instead of buying something to distract us temporarily from our feelings, the greatest gift we can give ourselves is reaching out to others for help or putting our circumstances into perspective by helping others in more challenging situations than ourselves.

- Liberating oneself from feeling attached to material possessions brings amazing freedom and a deeper connection to life.

Activity

Visiting Ecuador was one of the greatest trips I ever took because my luggage was lost. I was on a tight schedule and couldn't wait for the luggage to be found. So, I visited a market and got a few clothing items and toiletries that all fit in a small plastic shopping bag. I felt so free!

Think about something that you usually have with you at all times. Except for medicine, consider putting that precious item to the side for a few days as an exercise in liberating yourself from your possession.

Chapter 8

Corral Items To Free Your Mind

"I did not have three thousand pairs of shoes. I had one thousand and sixty."
— Imelda Marcos,
Former Philippines' First Lady

The key to liberating ourselves from clutter is to cease the inflow of unnecessary items. Often, it is our excitement in trying to get prepared to organize that can set us back. Have you ever decided to tackle an organizing project and the first thing you did was run out to buy containers or office supplies? We do that because the buying gives us the rush of feeling productive, and it also bides us a bit more time to distract ourselves from the very activity of clutterBusting!

When you put the pieces of the C.A.L.M. puzzle together in the order that I have outlined, it will save you time, energy and money. You might be asking yourself, "Why not have everything I need before I begin?" It's a valid question. I realize it might sound counterintuitive to delay buying the containers; however, you may not need as many containers as you initially think you do after you've separated your *Friends* from your *Strangers*.

At this stage of clutterBusting, you will have items consolidated, streamlined, and in the approximate vicinity you'd like them to reside. You are now better able to assess the shape, size, and number of appropriate containers in which to corral your belongings.

Corralling items is the best way to prevent sprawl, the first sign of clutter in the making. Corralling items helps us to have specific containers to keep things in. The key is to hold off on buying anything until you know how much of one category you have, where it is going, and what container will fit best in the space allotted. Corralling is equally if not more important for putting items away. Instead of throwing things in a drawer, you'll have a place in the drawer for paper clips, pens, keys, and so on.

Additionally, you may find items that you can repurpose as containers for corralling your items. Haven't you ever gotten home to start the project, and within a few hours you've abandoned the activity as well as all the containers? You then have a group of containers or file folders that now contribute to the clutter.

It's no secret that shopping is a mood booster. It literally releases dopamine, the happiness hormone. According to a 2011 survey taken in Britain by a shopping discount website, 40 percent of women acknowledged having up to five items of clothing hanging in their closets with the tags still attached. Paco Underhill, author of, *Why We Buy: The Science of Shopping* says, "*Two-thirds of the entire economy is impulse buying.*"

From the front door to the back door, think about all the activities that take place during the day in your home and where those activities take place.

For example....

- If your family takes off shoes at the front or back door and drops sports equipment there as well, then have a basket or cubby system to capture the items.

- Instead of throwing mail on the foyer table or keeping it in your hands as you walk through your home multi-tasking, have a specific box *inside* where mail is dropped to prevent the scattering of papers throughout the house. Make sure it is big enough to hold all the mail your family receives. Also, make sure that it is a mobile container, to enable you to move around with the mail, while always keeping documents within the box until you have handled the follow-up. You then have *one* place to find important mail items and you don't have to search your whole house trying to figure out where you put the insurance policy down when you were multi-tasking.

- For items that are going out the door with you—dry cleaning, a gift to drop off, a pair of shoes needing repair—have a tote at the front door to corral all those items. When you get home from your errands, use the tote to carry anything from your car that needs to go inside.

- Teach your children, early on, the importance of putting things back in their place by having named baskets on the stairs, or nearby, for them to bring their belongings back to their rooms. I implemented this for my client, Ann, and explained the concept to her children. She later told me her children began picking up their baskets and reciting "stow as you go" as they ascended the stairs. Just as children begin and end their days in bed, so must their belongings begin and end the day in their designated space.

My answer for HELP in families is this:

Have Everyone Learn to Pitch in.

- Instead of having all your linens in one closet, place your entertaining hand towels in the powder room, perhaps under the sink. This underscores the idea of putting items close to their point of use. Hand towels for your powder room is a category all its own.

- Invest in HIS and HERS toolboxes. A former beau gave me a fully equipped tool box for my birthday. While an untraditional gift for a woman, I still have it today. I love it and have put together these toolboxes for many of my clients. Keep picture hooks, furniture pads, a tape measure, screw driver, hammer, flashlight, and pair of scissors in it; this will also give these items, which typically get lost in the kitchen catchall drawer, a space of their own. Toolboxes are great because they are mobile.

- If your pantry or food cabinet has deep shelving, invest in Lazy Susans to make it easier to reach items. If the shelves are narrow, invest in tiered shelving racks so that you can stack more items in less space. Be mindful to group items by category when organizing your food area.

- Put drawer dividers in every drawer. This idea is not exclusive to kitchen drawers. I put these in bathroom drawers and dresser drawers to keep small items corralled and therefore neatly arranged. This idea is also beneficial when you're putting things back in their place. Instead of throwing them in their relegated drawer, they will now have a relegated place in the drawer.

- Keep trash bags in the bottom of trash cans. When one is full, you can easily pull it out and put a new one in immediately.

- Plastic food containers are best if you pick one or two sizes that make the most sense and stick to those sizes. Think of the concept of "one size fits all." It's easier to find a top and bottom that match. When not in use, they're easier to store one inside of another if they're all the same size. I recommend square shapes because they fit more easily in cabinets and drawers. If you already have many containers of varying sizes, give corresponding tops and bottoms a number to make it easier to find matches.

- Stackable shelving in traditionally large cabinet spaces, under the kitchen or bathroom sinks, keeps items arranged and easier to see. Cleaning supplies are also best arranged in handled containers for easy access to use; you can then return the whole container back to its designated space.

- If you still like to put pictures in photo albums, purchase a picture box to put them in until you have time to get them in the album. Inevitably, there may be pictures that you want to keep but no space in the album; if you have the picture box handy, then you can easily re-store the unused pictures in the box and label them. The best recommendation is to keep all your photos on CDs, and to create albums on-line.

- If you have more shoes than space on a shoe rack or cubby system, keep your nicer pairs in translucent boxes. You can then use a label maker to identify the shoes or place a picture of the shoes in the box that can be seen.

- For *Acquaintances*, like decorations, or items that you want to store for special occasions, for your children or grandchildren, I also recommend putting these items in translucent bins. When I was a child, I preferred open doors to allow me to always be able to see what was going on around me. Similarly, with translucent bins, you never again have to worry about approaching the mysterious brown box with trepidation about what may be looming inside.

- Remember to think about vertical storage. Hooks in closets are a wonderful way to keep items from ending up on the floor and will most likely save you money at the cleaners. When deciding what to wear, instead of throwing 'the no's' on the bed, put them on a hanger on a pop-down bar attached to the door or wall in your closet. Then, when you have more time, you can easily slide them back into their appropriate place in your well categorized closet. I am a big proponent of over-the-door hook racks, so clients can move them around if necessary.

- Painted peg boards are a fun way to display items and create a visual aesthetic, especially when you want to teach your children how to return things into their assigned places.

- Repurpose items to surround yourself with "functional art" pieces that you don't have space to display, but you'd like to see. Use decorative bowls or baskets for small items that look messy when thrown into a drawer. Keep your mouthwash bottle in a beautiful ceramic vase to hide the mouthwash and enjoy your art piece every day. I use a small decorative vase in my refrigerator that hides the baking soda.

I am continually asked if creative people are just naturally messy. My answer is NO. Before starting my organizing business, friends urged me to consider becoming a designer. I am recognized as a creative individual, and I understand the desire to SEE things. I use open shelving for clothing that most people put in drawers. Armoires with shelves also work well. I keep a smaller hanging file on my desk where I can easily contain my "active" papers while also seeing them. There are definitely ways to create organizational systems to work with every kind of personality.

Corralling is critical for the creation of calm environments. When items have their personal space, it's more evident to us when things are out of place. It's a huge motivation to keep things in order. With items in containers, baskets, and decorative bins, there is less visual stuff that the eye has to capture and process, allowing our brains to relax.

Let's think about the difference between a hook full of purses in varying shapes, sizes and colors that bombards the eye as each one vies for attention every time you open your closet versus a basket placed on a shelf that contains the same purses. While the former example might not necessarily be clutter, the second example offers a calmer picture with less distraction.

Just as we thoughtfully corral and contain items that are seen daily in our homes, we must remember to carefully "restore" our items in drawers and closets. Whether displayed or stored, items that share space in our home belong to us and must be attended to. It is a responsibility we accept when we carry them across the threshold of our nest.

"If we care ABOUT our items, then we need to care FOR them; as we care for them, we care for ourselves.

— Virginia Barkley

Summary Points

- Corralling items prevents them from sprawling. Especially for small items that can get jumbled in drawers, corralling is essential to keep categories of items from mingling.

- Before buying any containers, it's critical to know what you're going to put in them and where they are going to be placed.

- Be creative with your corralling containers—repurposing decorative boxes, bowls and vases that you already have but are not using.

Activity

Choose one category of items that have gotten caught in the clutter. After consolidating the items and choosing the *Friends* that will remain, think about where to store the items. Then, choose a container that will fit into the designated space and corral all the items within the category.

Maintain

Part Four - The Final Piece Of The Puzzle

Chapter 9

Embrace Change
(And modify if necessary)

> "Always bear in mind that your own resolution to succeed is more important than any one thing."

— Abraham Lincoln

ClutterBusting is like getting into shape. Once you reach your desired results, it's still necessary to do a little something every day that makes it easier to keep your environment working for you.

Once a clutterBusting project has been completed, it's only natural that it may initially feel strange. Energy has been jostled. Give yourself time to live with the changes for a while. If, after a few weeks, something isn't feeling right or you notice that one item is continually ending up in a different place, then make the change that makes you feel better. **Modify and move on.**

Modifying is the action that seeks to improve upon what's been set into motion. Remaining aware of your surroundings, and keeping both your environment and your activities in alignment with your life's vision, is essential to maintaining your newly organized spaces. ClutterBusting is like losing weight; if you don't maintain, you're going to gain the clutter back.

Celebrating your success and enjoying your accomplishments are also important. Focusing on how much better your environment looks and feels will feed your momentum to keep things in their place. It's a very dangerous detour to start questioning your capabilities and sliding into believing that something is not working and therefore it can't work. Recognize what you have achieved and realize that you have made progress. Being in tune with your surroundings, noticing what is working and what is not working, is part of *being* organized.

You are the master of your things; they only overwhelm you when you allow them to. You have the power of choice, the power to choose how you handle challenges: boxing gloves, drama club, off to the races, or garden party (chapter one reference). As author Robert Fulgam writes, "*One of life's best coping mechanisms is to know the difference between an inconvenience and a problem. Life is inconvenient. Life is lumpy. A lump in the oatmeal, a lump in the throat and a lump in the breast are not the same kind of lump. One needs to learn the difference.*"

Are you expending your time and energy on inconveniences or problems? If your answer is *inconveniences*, then my next question is this: What is the overriding feeling associated with these inconveniences? The answer is usually that which is being buried under the clutter.

Thoughtful Organization is being mindful of our environments both at and away from home and realizing that all choices we make affect all areas of our lives. It's inevitable that things will get out of place from time to time; it's called LIFE and it happens in my home as well.

Being organized means that while things may get out of place, we can easily whip our homes into shape because:

- our belongings have a designated place;
- we practice organizational skills daily;
- we are committed to our mental health and well-being;
- we ask for help when we need it, and;
- we live an abundant life full of love, joy, peace, patience, kindness, goodness, faithfulness, gentleness, and self-control (Galatians 5:22); when our lives are full of those, there's no room for the clutter anymore!

Congratulations for taking action, investing in yourself by committing to busting through whatever clutter is literally weighing you down and holding you back. It's time to reclaim your space, time, and energy and to embrace every moment of life with gratitude, hopefulness, enthusiasm, and trust.

"Cherish your visions; cherish your ideals;
cherish the music that stirs in your heart,
the beauty that forms in your mind,
the loveliness that drapes your purest thoughts,
for out of them will grow delightful conditions,
all heavenly environment; of these, if you but
remain true to them your world will at last be built."

— James Allen,
British philosophical writer,
best known for his book,
As A ManThinketh

Summary Points

- Keeping our homes organized is just like keeping our teeth clean; we have to attend to our things to prevent clutter, or plaque, from building up.

- Celebrating both the clutterBusting success and the maintenance of your newly organized spaces is key to keeping the momentum high.

- It's imperative that you continually and strongly believe in your capabilities to clutterBust your spaces and to make changes when necessary to ensure the maintenance of your organized spaces.

Activity

Invest in yourself and track the value of every day by writing in a Gratitude Journal. Each night, write about the events from your day for which you are most grateful. By writing at night, you'll begin to think throughout the day about what will be going into the journal and therefore stay more focused and aware of the delights in your day rather than the inconveniences.

Chapter 10

Add Environmental CALM to Your Daily 'Must Have List'

"The experiences of life hold more value than that which we tether ourselves to in the form of clutter."

— Virginia Barkley

The key to maintaining peaceful environments is integrating your organizational activities into other daily actions that you consistently take. **Thoughtful Organization is not a state of doing but a state of being that complements the**

rhythm of our lives. Just as important to our well-being as eating or sleeping is remaining aware and respectful of the condition of our most sacred home environment from which we operate our lives.

The purpose and benefit of thoughtfully organizing our homes is that it allows our brains to feel more relaxed both when we're looking for things as well as when we're putting objects back where they belong. When organized, our home becomes our ally, acting as a buoy to lift us up and keep us afloat when unexpected situations arise.

The more consistent we are with the maintenance of our organizational creations, the more we will trust the process and feel confident about immediately putting our hands on items that we need. We experience renewed energy because we're expending less of it on worrying that something is lost, or running around in circles trying to remember where we put the $\underline{X}$ the last time we used it!

If you pick something up, remain focused on that particular item until you've put it in its place. The key is to not pick up something else if you already have something in your hands, unless the second item is going to the same place. I call this activity **Practicing Presence**.

Being organized is settling into a new and healthier habit of ensuring that belongings have a home within your home and that they make their way back to those homes by day's end. My recommendation is that you recognize the importance of self-care.

A necessary part of self-care is the creation of a C.A.L.M environment. If our bodies are gifted houses for our souls, then our homes are merely extensions of our bodies and thus another representation of the condition of our souls. What is your soul saying to you when you look around your home?

Maintaining our environment is merely the consistent exercising of our awareness muscle, most notably our eyes and our consciousness, to prevent the experiences of our days from numbing us to our surroundings. If we are focusing on chaos, we'll get chaos. If we are focusing on being scattered and out of control, then we will remain scattered and out of control. However, if we focus on staying grounded, confident in our capabilities, and consistent in our efforts, no matter what situation presents itself, we will meet it with surprising, delightful success.

Maintaining our environment also includes continually streamlining items out of our life that no longer serve a purpose for us. I want you to read the following declaration three times:

> I am not responsible for finding the perfect
> home for my *Strangers.*

> My only responsibility is to decide whether to
> keep items or donate them.

> The donation site will then decide what to do
> with my *Strangers.*

Organizing is not only an achievable skill but, more importantly, a fun and fruitful activity where the harvest you reap is full of peaceful and functional environments from which you will emerge recharged, rejuvenated, and reconnected to the truest form of life's abundance... MORE LIVING and less stuff.

Conclusion

"You must learn a new way to think
before you can master a new way to be."

— Marianne Williamson,
Spiritual activist, author, and
founder of The Peace Alliance

I did not write this book as a passive reference for readers to try their hand, yet again, at organizing their belongings. I wrote this book to be used as an active roadmap for those of you who have had enough of your encroaching stuff. Disorganization does not merit the drama it provides in our lives.

Our primitive instinct gives us two choices when we are fearful: fight or flight. Closing doors or filling time with distractions undermines our confidence. Distraction is not escape, but rather the exact opposite. **Distraction is what builds the bars between us and our goals and dreams**.

My C.A.L.M. philosophy for busting through mental, emotional and physical clutter has helped thousands of people accomplish the goals they set out to achieve.

I am on a mission to shift the mindset of abundance from the world of accumulating things to the infinite and joy-filled world of connecting more deeply with others, savoring life experiences, respecting our emotions, and accepting more fully the richness that lies within ourselves, which will continue to transform our lives until our last day. The fewer things we choose to juggle, the greater the quality of our days as more time is being invested in rewarding pursuits. **The more clutter in our lives, the more diluted our enjoyment of life becomes**.

Ancient Egyptians made an art of accumulating possessions because they believed their possessions would go with them into the afterlife. My C.A.L.M philosophy is based on my belief that we take none of our possessions with us when we exit this world.

I was working at *The Coca-Cola Company* when its longtime CEO, Roberto Goizueta, died. At church the following Sunday, the minister said that many people had approached him and asked how much Mr. Goizueta had left behind. His answer was simple and profound: "He left it all."

Delighting in and cultivating one's presence in the now, embracing the fullness of every day no matter what we're doing, living in communion with people rather than things is what I hope this book will help women achieve by removing clutter from their lives. Everyone deserves peace.

I have come to appreciate the exercise of awareness while walking through the rooms of my home. We live in an era of unprecedented abundance with marketers doing their best to convince us that there is still something that we lack. Believing there is lack prevents us from seeing what is physically in front of us. **Belief in our abundance starts when we are able to fully appreciate and focus on what we have versus what we think we need.**

ClutterBusting is worth every bit of the time it takes in the beginning in order to move to a more grounded place from which you can assess all of your opportunities and make decisions about which direction you choose to steer your life and your time. It's a human right to live in a calm environment, to be nurtured by and relaxed in our homes.

Since I am convinced that the world is spinning faster on its axis, I believe it's critical to our health and well-being to be able to step out of our front doors feeling calm and grounded versus frazzled and manic by 8am! It is equally important that when we arrive home after a full day, we feel happy and at peace in our surroundings.

The top 10 situations or experiences that cause stress are: childhood trauma, personal relationships, death, divorce, employment, finances, health, pregnancy, a chronically ill child, and moving. I believe *clutter* is No.11 and that, when present, it exponentially increases the stress factor of the previous 10 stress-inducing situations.

There are plenty of ways we outwardly manifest stress in our lives: clenching our jaws, biting our nails, feeling scattered, losing our patience and perhaps our temper, and allowing clutter to grow. Simultaneously, our bodies are bearing our stress, possibly causing: a compromised immune system, indigestion, kidney stones, tumors, cancer, and a host of other diseases.

With so many illnesses whose causes remain unknown, the dis-ease that clutter creates is something that can be addressed and eliminated from our lives. We must give ourselves permission to just stop and have some time to think, to take a deep breath, to be still for a moment, to listen to what we need emotionally, and to feel confident that we can not only get it but that it's worth the pursuit. Seeking out both the knowledge and insights of those with more experience can move us closer to our goals more quickly.

My passion is helping people lift the veil of clutter and confusion and embrace life more fully and confidently by putting my C.A.L.M philosophy into practice with purpose, playfulness, and perseverance.

Life is like a Ferris wheel. Whether you're seated at the top or circling the bottom, you can decide to enjoy every part of the ride. The most important decision we make is choosing to get on and take a ride.

"Take a risk on yourself and expect to be delightfully surprised."

— Virginia Barkley

Acknowledgements

I am truly blessed to be able to support women and help them achieve greater success while doing something that I love. I am further blessed by the support of people who love what they do and have worked beside me to make this book a success. There's no time like the present, right James?

I also want to thank my awesome clients for trusting me and to congratulate you for having the courage to persevere through the clutterBusting process and emerging refreshed and more confident about your organizing capabilities, on the other side. I count you among my friends.

To my fellow colleagues of The National Association Of Professional Organizers (NAPO), with whom I've continued to hone my knowledge and skills. I feel blessed to be part of an industry dedicated to transforming chaos into calm, and bringing greater peace into the lives of others.

Thank you to Kim Hodous and Matt Patterson, two incredible friends to me while navigating this part of my journey. My love and gratitude for each of you runs deep.

T.Harv Eker, there are no words to express my love for you and appreciation for your life's work. You are a giant among men, and I am not sure where I'd be right now had I not, but for the grace of God, been introduced to and transformed by your experiential teaching. AHO!

Constance and Charlotte, you mean the world to me. Your support, participation, and enthusiasm to see me succeed is indeed, part of my success.

Mom and Dad, my love for you is beyond measure. Thank you so much for your generous hearts.

And mom, well...all I can say is, you're irreplaceable—as a mother, friend, business advisor, marketing director, ideas brainstormer and No.1 cheerleader. The countless hours we've spent together on my business have been priceless in wisdom, laughter, and sheer fun. You are, truly, the greatest.

Until next time......

Speaking Engagements

If you enjoyed, *ClutterBusting for Busy Women*
Virginia Barkley
Is The Ideal Professional Speaker
For Your Next Event!
"America's Leading Authority on
clutterBusting for Busy Women"

Virginia Barkley is a sought-after speaker who will leave your audience energized, empowered, and excited to immediately start busting through the stuff that clutters their lives. Her humor, high energy and passion are contagious and will not only delight, but will deliver a simple message that will result in swift positive change.

Virginia believes that everyone has the capacity to clutterBust. She says, *"The question is not whether you're capable of clutterBusting; the question is whether you will open yourself up to learning and personal growth."*

If you would like to know more about booking Virginia for a keynote, breakout or workshop, please contact our office at 504.615.2678, or email questions to: virginia@ClutterBustingForBusyWomen.com

Share this Book!

Quantity discounts available.

Personalized, autographed copies also available.

Contact Us For A Quote!

Addendum

"Not what we have but what we
enjoy constitutes our abundance."

— John Petit-Senn, French poet

Barry Izsak, a former president of NAPO and an organizer
with whom I have worked, has been quoted as saying,
"Doctors save lives and we change lives. We're not a luxury
service. We're a necessity. We truly have an impact on
humanity. How many can say that at the end of the day?"

Individuals and families pay a high price for tolerating
clutter and remaining disorganized. Clutter is an epidemic,
especially in the United States. According to www.
selfstorage.org, 79 percent of storage facilities worldwide
are located in the United States (2009). Yet, 80 percent of
what we keep is rarely used (Agency Sales Magazine).

The following statistics underscore the prevalence of
disorganization and stuff mismanagement in our society.

Sixty-five percent of people describe themselves as "very" or "insanely" busy.

– Day Runner Survey

Sixty-eight percent of Americans say they need to improve their organizational skills.

– 2011 OfficeMax Survey

Fifty-three percent of Americans admit they think less of co-workers who have messy desks, while forty percent say a co-worker's cluttered workspace makes them assume the person is lacking in other aspects of their job.

– 2011 OfficeMax Survey

Thirty-five percent of Americans admit they are ashamed of anyone seeing their desk or workspace while twenty-eight percent said they are ashamed to let someone see their bedrooms.

– 2011 OfficeMax Survey

Eighty-five percent of the papers filed are never looked at again.

– Small Business Administration

Twenty-three percent of adults pay bills late and incur fees because they can't find their bills.

– Harris Interactive, American market research
company

The average American burns fifty-five minutes a day looking for things they know they have but can't find.

– *Newsweek*

Twenty-five percent of people with two-car garages fill it with too much stuff that they can't park a car inside.

– U.S. Department of Energy

The cure?
Keep C.A.L.M.
and carry on.

16845202R00081

Made in the USA
Charleston, SC
13 January 2013